MW01288718

SLAIN
IN THE
Spirit

SLAIN
IN THE
Spirit

*It's not about falling down,
it's about getting up.*

SYLVIA CORBIN HALL

XULON PRESS

Xulon Press
2301 Lucien Way #415
Maitland, FL 32751
407.339.4217
www.xulonpress.com

© 2021 by Sylvia Corbin Hall

All rights reserved solely by the author. The author guarantees all contents are original and do not infringe upon the legal rights of any other person or work. No part of this book may be reproduced in any form without the permission of the author.

Due to the changing nature of the Internet, if there are any web addresses, links, or URLs included in this manuscript, these may have been altered and may no longer be accessible. The views and opinions shared in this book belong solely to the author and do not necessarily reflect those of the publisher. The publisher therefore disclaims responsibility for the views or opinions expressed within the work.

Unless otherwise indicated, Scripture quotations taken from the King James Version (KJV) – *public domain.*

Scripture quotations taken from the New American Standard Bible (NASB). Copyright © 1960, 1962, 1963, 1968, 1971, 1972, 1973, 1975, 1977, 1995 by The Lockman Foundation. Used by permission. All rights reserved.

Scripture quotations taken from the Holy Bible, New International Version (NIV). Copyright © 1973, 1978, 1984, 2011 by Biblica, Inc.™. Used by permission. All rights reserved.

Paperback ISBN-13: 978-1-66283-523-0
Ebook ISBN-13: 978-1-66283-524-7

TABLE OF CONTENTS

Acknowledgements

Thank you Charlie, Kevin, Anthony, Jamie, Eric, Ramon, Sean and Lisa for being the best kids in the whole world. You have given me so much joy and encouragement in all that I have done. Going back to school at the age of 45 was not easy but you always let me know that I could do it. You have provided me with years of wonderful memories. How we would sit around the table after dinner, all the jokes and sharing events of the day, or were you just delaying doing the dishes. What a wild bunch we have always been! Our home was founded on the word of God, filled with discipline and love, and purposed to give you wings.

Thank you Jeannie, JoAnn, Nora, Sheila and Veronica for all those fantastic Monday night "girls for God" evenings we shared. Wow, did we see God show up!

Thank you Glenda Moser, therapist extraordinaire, who patiently and lovingly walked with me through one of the most traumatic years of my life.

THANK YOU GOD, for choosing and using me!

INTRODUCTION

Today, in the Christian community, there is a great debate regarding being "slain in the spirit". Some say that this is emotionalism. I wholeheartedly agree. Yet, how can I not become emotional when I realize that God:

Who spoke the world into existence,

Who is all powerful, present everywhere and all knowing,

Who knows my past, present and future sins, yet loves me with a passion known only by Him,

Who sent His ONLY son to die in my place so that I can share in all the glory that is rightfully His

Who will give me eternal life with Him, if I submit my life and will to Him,

Who loves me and longs to spend time with me,

Who has promised to save and change me from the wretched creature that I am and to give me His Holy Spirit,

Who causes me to be victorious through Him, no matter what Satan sends my way?

Who forgives me over and over again for my mistakes and my sins.

I THINK THAT'S SOMETHING TO GET
EMOTIONAL ABOUT!

I don't know how the descriptive phrase "slain in the spirit" originated, but I have seen men, women, boys and girls, after they have been prayed for, do some really strange stuff. I've seen some whose hands begin to violently vibrate, some swished back and forth like an old fashioned washing machine, some laughed, some cried, and some just fell prostrate on the floor. I couldn't imagine losing my composure and allowing something so bizarre to happen to me. It seemed so UNDIGNIFIED! Sometimes people weren't even touched and they would crumple to the floor. I even observed a few fall forward on their faces.

"Is it real?" I wondered. As I watched other people experience being "slain in the spirit" I would mentally attempted to judge which were real, which could possibly be flesh, or which were just plain phony. But one thing I was sure of, I WANTED NO PART OF IT!

Come along on a journey with me as I learn, it's not as much about what happens when you fall down, it's about what happens after you get up.

Chapter 1

SET UP TO FALL

Attending church had not been a part of my husband's upbringing and for me church was just a social event. It was about youth choir, Christmas and Easter pageants, scripture memory contest etc. but very little teaching on having a personal relationship with God. As the old saying goes "going to church doesn't make you Christian any more than sleeping in a garage makes you a car". At the age of 21 I had a personal encounter with the living God and strangely enough it was due to my unsaved husband.

As I struggled to raise our eight children in a Godly home the Holy Spirit would teach me how to first be a woman of God, then a Godly wife and mother. Having been raised in a single parent home where there was no model of Godliness, the Holy Spirit had a lot of work to do in both my husband and me. I was hungry for more of the Holy Spirit. I started attending the church I grew up in but they weren't comfortable with all my questions. So the search was on for a church where I felt comfortable. For 5 years I visited various churches and denominations, and I happened to drive past a church where I saw a familiar name on the sign in front of the church. The Pastor and his brother had been a part of the Charismatic Renewal in Pittsburgh. I felt like it was a "God speak" moment when you

1

know that what just happened was no accident. The following Sunday I attended that Church. People seemed to be rushing to get inside. I thought I must be late but as I entered I felt such a powerful anointing. That same anointing was on the music and the message. I went home and told my husband about all I had experienced. I knew this was where God would have me but I asked God for a fleece like Gideon. I prayed "God if this is where you would have me, please have my husband attend church with me. My husband had only attended church when the children were participating in something. I would come home every Sunday bubbling over with excitement about how powerful the word was and how more and more people were attending. I kept praying and attending sharing all I had heard and learned and how Holy Spirit was doing a work in my life. I don't know whether my husband saw a change or whether he was just tired of my nagging so he finally said yes. Not only did he attend that Sunday but within a year we joined the church. Our God does exceedingly, abundantly above all we can ask or think!

This journey of mine started in the spring of 1995. One of the exciting things about being a part of Covenant Church of Pittsburgh is the powerfully anointed men and women of God who come and share their gifts with us. Among those were the Harfouches, a husband and wife team whose home ministry is located in Florida. After sharing their testimony and the word of God with us, they asked if there was anyone who wanted prayer to come forward. Who doesn't want prayer. My issue was walking up front. That is where my journey began. About ten people stood immediately. The first few people were prayed for and they returned to their seats. Some were crying, some were smiling but one crumpled to the floor. At this season in my Christian walk I found it difficult to raise my hands higher than shoulder level, much less stand and walk up front in the presence of six or seven hundred people. I was so insecure and intimidated I felt uncomfortable in a stadium with thousands of other people, standing to salute the flag. Hey, I'm 6' 2"! I stand out even when I am seated.

I sat in my seat going through an enormous battle. I thought, if this really is of God I don't want to miss this experience. My spirit said "GO, GO!" My mind said "NO, NO!" I finally decided, "Why not." I had "a plan." If I chickened out I could always just sit down in the nearest seat and pretend that I just wanted a closer seat. The odds were slim that I'll be the one in ten that ends up on the floor. "I can do this", I told myself. I stood up to get in line. As I reached mid-aisle, twenty or thirty other people got the same revelation, and before I knew it, I was sandwiched in the middle of what seemed to be a sea of people. Why is it that you never think of Plan B until Plan A has failed?

There was now no turning back. Now everyone who was prayed for was ending up on the floor. SET UP BY THE HOLY SPIRIT! I quickly started working on Plan B. "Okay, okay, just be cool", I told myself. My only experience with fainting was as a teenager, after being in a hot home economics class, I suddenly stood up and the next thing I remember I was in the nursing office lying on a cot. I assumed this would be a similar experience. You fall down, become unconscious, then you wake up.

The creation of a Plan B was interrupted by one of the pastors beckoning me to come on the pulpit because by this time the aisles were covered with bodies. Okay now it's time to go to Plan C!!!! When they touch me I'll just raise my hands, maybe, and then make a quick retreat to my seat. I'm not sure if anyone touched me, I just found myself on the floor, arms extended, looking up at the ceiling. I could hear and see all that was going on around me. Soon the entire pulpit was covered with bodies also. I'm thinking, "closed eyes are better, maybe even more spiritual. Well at least I won't be able to see

3

if people are watching me". I lay there for awhile waiting for unconsciousness to overcome me. NOTHING!

I could sense that it was really getting crowded on the pulpit. The Harfouches had moved to the rear of the sanctuary. From the floor in the rear of the sanctuary, I heard someone laughing as if they had just heard the funniest joke ever. The voice sounded familiar. I opened my eyes just enough to peek at what was going on, but not enough for anyone to notice that I was conscious. It was my husband! Now I notice some of the folks on the floor are writhing, but I have never felt so relaxed or so at peace, but I knew I could not stay there forever. Then it occurred to me, "How am I going to gracefully extricate myself from what is now an ocean of people?" As I said, I'm 6' 2" and grace was never one of my strong points. It is rumored that your arms length is approximately the same as your height, so with my arms extended the space I'm taking up is probably the space of two people. So as any thoughtful person would do, I decided to move my arms down to my sides. Nothing happened! It felt as though my arms weighed a ton. I tried again. Nothing. I tried again. Nothing. Okay God, what is going on here? I attempted to move a leg. Nothing. The other leg. Nothing. My arms and legs are frozen to the floor!

At this point I open my eyes wide. My intellect immediately tried to sort this out. I'm a nurse, so I do an assessment. Confusion, sensory changes, altered levels of consciousness, paralysis. STROKE! Suddenly all thoughts of embarrassment was gone. I looked for someone to help me. My nurses training and experience had taught me that the sooner a stroke victim is treated, the better the chances of survival. To my amazement there is not a vertical person except the pianist on the pulpit. All the aisles are covered with prostrate bodies manifesting some pretty weird stuff. I attempt to form the word "HELP" and all that comes out is "ummmmph". Again I attempt to yell the word "help", UMMMMMMMMMMPH! My lips felt like they weighed a ton also. My mind envisions my future. Me, the big dummy who goes for prayer to experience a closer walk with God is about to have that final walk with God.

I knew I should feel panicky but again an overpowering feeling of peace engulfed me. I just laid there enjoying this feeling of euphoria. After what seemed like an hour, but was probably minutes, a pastor very gingerly picked up one of my arms and then the other and placed them at my sides. Whoa! I'm back in business. I consider getting up and returning to my seat. Guess what? Those same arms that Pastor Bob had no problem moving to my sides are now frozen there at my sides. Once more that blanket of peace covered me from head to toe and I lay there not wanting to ever loose that feeling.

Just as suddenly as the power that caused me to be unable to move came, it was gone and I was able to move my arms and legs. I could feel this silly grin on my face but I couldn't stop smiling. What seemed like a movie played in slow motion, I rolled over on my side, got up on my knees, then one foot and the other, and finally pushed until I was in a standing position. This standing process probably took a few minutes. Trying to gather all the decorum I could, on legs that seemed to be made of gelatin, (I'm sure I looked like a poor imitation of Charlie Chaplin), I staggered to the nearest pew, sat for quite a while reveling in this new-found euphoria, oblivious of what was going on around me, before returning to my seat.

For weeks afterward I basked in this marvelous experience going over it again and again in my mind, hopelessly trying to rationalize what had occurred. I didn't realize at that time, that falling down was the easy part. What happens after that is the challenge.

Chapter II

Do you trust me?

I t was Labor Day 1995, a holiday when our children, who are scattered across the country, are usually able to gather together. That is when the following scenario began. My husband, Charles, and my 40th wedding anniversary, March 11th, and our 60th birthdays were approaching. Our children decided they wanted to surprise us and do something special for us. We would overhear them asking each other what they thought about various ways to commemorate these events. We overheard them say "banquet". We prayed, Aruba! Someone else mentioned a second wedding ceremony with all the trimmings. Our first wedding was in the Pastor's study with just a few family members attending. We prayed "Bahamas". Don't get me wrong, all of those things were nice but we could see ourselves being so caught up in THEIR plans that by the time the event occurred, we would probably be too exhausted to enjoy it. We were also concerned that they may forget someone and they would be offended.

After much prayer on OUR part, they finally asked us what WE would like to do. Ten years earlier we had been to the Bahamas and had become friends with some very nice people who lived there. We had often mentioned to our children how much we wanted to return. Knowing this, with a sigh of relief we very nonchalantly said, "Oh, a little getaway trip would be nice". They said, "Great! We will do all the planning. You just prepare to go". After they had left, the minuscule amount of our Native American heritage took on an enormous dimension as we did a celebration dance that would have made our ancestors proud!

As Thanksgiving and Christmas approached, as custom would have it, those who couldn't come home for one holiday would be home for the other. We made sure we prepared everyone's favorite foods. After all, our wonderful, precious, generous, delightful, kind and thoughtful kids are planning a special trip for us. "Oh, you'd like deviled eggs? Both kinds? Banana Nut Bread? Banana Split Cake? Would I bake cookies? No problem. Fresh greens which I had only made a few times. Fresh greens which have to rinsed in **_COLD_** salt water numerous times with these arthritic fingers? That's pushing it but, okay, after all these marvelous creatures we have given life to, educated, and have been the focal point of our life, are planning a wonderful, relaxing vacation for us. What's a little sacrifice for these thoughtful kids of ours. I could almost feel the intensity of the Bahamian sun. Visions of basking in the sun, reading all those books I've been meaning to read, listening to the sound of the waves gently caressing the beach, blending magnificently with Scriabin (my favorite) or Mozart (Charles's favorite) coming from our portable tape recorder, as he painted awesome seascapes.

With the holidays behind us and our anniversary rapidly approaching, we started some strategic planning of our own. For Christmas, Paul Gruver, a friend of Charles, had given him a really neat portable easel with paints and brushes which he planned to take along with several canvases. We joked about how the airport security might confiscate this suitcase because of its questionable contents. Remembering how expensive articles like sunscreen, lotion and other personal items were in the Islands I made sure my cosmetic case was filled with everything we might possibly need for a sun-filled vacation. Thank heaven I had made long skirts to match my bathing suits, which I planned would be my major day-time attire. After sixty years of living, the process of time and gravity has made some very noticeable alterations to my anatomy. I planned on taking one fancy dress and one dinner jacket for Charles for that one special evening when we would go to some elegant, super-chic restaurant where we would pretend we lived this lifestyle all the time. There would be many island meals in small Bahamian fami-ly-style restaurants and roadside eateries where we would just "chill" and get to know the residents.

We tried not to notice an excessive number of long distance calls that our daughter, Lisa, made to North Carolina, New York City, and Rochester, New York where some of our children live. When those who lived in Pittsburgh would suddenly become quiet whenever Charles or I would approach them we would smile, giving each other a knowing look, that we had probably interrupted some of their strategic very hush-hush planning. "What wonderful kids," we thought.

Two weeks before our anniversary, our daughter Lisa, who has always had to fight for recognition from her seven older brothers, informed us that she had designated herself as spokesperson for our trip. She's excited. We're apprehensive. Didn't her brothers remember that this is the same person who, on the eve of her tenth birthday, her brother Jamie told her (with a straight face) that she had to stay awake until midnight or she would change into a boy. He said he and all six of his brothers had started out as girls but they could not stay awake until midnight and had turned into boys. AND SHE BELIEVED HIM! She said she had planned our trip, (we've got the greatest kids in the world), hotel reservations were made (great organization!), a rental car arranged (nice touch) and a generous daily stipend provided (what were we worried about?). Although it was a cold blustery February day in Pittsburgh, we could almost visualize the clear, vibrant blue water and white sandy beaches surrounding the islands, envision the verdant countryside, feel the warmth of the sun caressing our aging bodies, taste the conch salad (one of Charles's favorite island dishes sold in the marketplaces). Our senses had kicked into overdrive. We were floating in a bubble of ecstasy and expectation! She said her brothers wanted us to go back to the Bahamas, BUT (with that 'but" we simultaneously felt the bubble burst over our head). She said she had heard us discussing the Airport Vineyard Church phenomena and she felt led to make arrangements for us to spend a week in TORONTO! She felt led? She felt LED? Whatever led her, couldn't it lead her south instead of north? Sabotaged by our only daughter. My first thought was, "I love Toronto with its friendly people, gigantic shopping mall, its beautiful historic sights, its cleanness BUT March isn't a time of year I'd normally want to vacation in Canada. Secondly, I was curious as to whether what was happening there was of God, was this for everyone or for a select few and for what purpose?" Inquiring minds want to know. Our pastors and several members of our church had been there and came back with glowing reports of how the Holy Spirit was operating there. Thirdly, I wouldn't have a need for sunscreen, bathing suits and definitely not a halter top chiffon dress. A major wardrobe adjustment was our new priority. What do you wear to a church that, at that time, had been meeting every day for fifteen months; where people come from all over the world? Oh well, what harm will it do just to check it out. Who knows, I may be just sitting in my chair singing and praising God and the Holy Spirit may touch my vocal chords and mellifluous sounds may just begin emanating from me. The people around me will be amazed at this marvelous transformation. I love to sing but

I can't carry a tune. Maybe I'll just be sitting in my chair and lean over to touch someone in a wheelchair and they leap up and start walking. Visions of Kathryn Kuhlman float through my head. My mother and I use to attend her services in Pittsburgh and I was always impressed by her. I promised myself though, no more of that going up front stuff. After all, God knows where I am. Right?

As we set off from Pittsburgh for our Canadian adventure, we reminisced about our yearly summer vacations at Lake Erie when the children were young. It still amazes us how we were able to spend three hours in a station wagon with eight squirming kids.

One year we extended our vacation to include Niagara Falls doing all the usual tourist-y things visiting the wax museum, playing miniature golf, going up in the revolving observation tower, as well as taking in the breathtaking grandeur of the falls.

As we neared Toronto, our minds went back to our last visit to this grand city. Our son Kevin ("Harry and the Hendersons") and Tom Hanks were filming "Mazes and Monsters" in this city about ten years earlier. At that time Tom Hanks was just beginning his career. He was also going to school at that time and spent most of his free time studying. When we see this marvelous actor now we say, "We've met him!" It was our first opportunity to personally share in our son's acting career. Kevin died April 11, 1991 of A.I.D.S. related illnesses. Bittersweet memories consume our senses, which caused us to spend the rest of the trip to Toronto in silence.

At the Royal Constellation Hotel, we discovered that many guests were also there to be a part of the "Toronto Blessing". There was an air of expectancy that was infectious. After unpacking we just hung out in the lobby soaking in the ambiance. Later that day we grabbed a quick dinner and headed for the Airport Vineyard Church. We were an hour early and yet there was a line from all entrances winding through the vestibule to the sidewalk. Strangers were introducing themselves, laughing and talking as though they had known each other for years. Time seemed to rapidly pass and soon we were in the sanctuary. My first observation was that it was no ordinary looking church. There were no stained glass windows, no pews, no crosses, no choir loft, no fancy architectural eye pleasers, yet that air of expectancy was even greater once we were inside. There was no rushing to find a seat, it was as if God had called us here and He already had everything worked out so where we sat or who sat next to whom was predetermined. As we waited for the service to begin, I glanced around at the faces of those seated near us. It was as if we were in a meeting at the United Nations. It seemed as though there were a dozen languages being spoken around us. Many of the people had what looked like small transistor radios, which I later discovered were translating machines.

My home church is known for its powerful worship and praise. As worship began the first thing that struck me was, the words were not familiar in many of the songs, yet the moving of the Holy Spirit was just as powerful. In no time at all I felt a special anointing in the building. People were doing some pretty unusual things and no one had touched them. I thought to myself, "There's no way I'm going to go up front in this crowd!" I saw a blond young lady who seemed to have some malady that made her jerk and bend over like a chicken walking. Behind her was a young man who seemed to the same malady only in a lesser form. Following them was a group who made sounds that reminded me of the grunts and groans of the labor pains of my last son who tipped the scales at 10 lbs. and 10 oz. I thought, "How nice, they have brought in people from some institution". As they approached the platform, I soon found out that this was the worship team and this behavior was only manifested under the anointing of the Holy Spirit. So many new things were going on around me, yet in the midst of it all there remained an air of expectancy. It was like the feeling you get when you are in an electric storm. Actually the hair on my arms stood up and I got goosebumps. I remember wondering if Charles and the rest of the people were feeling the same excitement. Someone on the platform asked where we were from and there were people from England, many European countries, South America, Japan, China, all across the United States, and from one end of Canada to the other, yet there was feeling of unity in the praise and worship. It has never been more evident to me that the Holy Spirit goes beyond, and is not limited to our language, location or ethnicity. The main emphasis was on praising and worshiping God. Then the word was given. I don't remember the exact scriptures but the subject was about encouraging the people of God to learn to hear the voice of God. It was very motivational.

It was getting late and I was thinking, "Wow! I can't wait to get back to the hotel and get some sleep so I will be fresh and alert for tomorrow's sessions," but it wasn't over. The leader now said that all those who wanted prayer should go to the rear where they had placed rows and rows of mats. Would you believe at least one third off the people headed for the rear of the church? Charles was one of the first ones back there. I never got a chance to remind him of what had happened at our church. Well, I certainly wasn't going to make a spectacle of myself again, especially in the presence of all these strangers. I would just sit this one out. I turned around and sure enough they were dropping like flies back there. They made what went on back at Covenant seem like nursery school. People were crying, some were bent forward, some were bent backward, some just stood but many of them looked like they were frozen to the floor. I sat in my chair and read my bible trying to look super spiritual for a while, then I struck up a conversation with a woman from Germany. She had been saving all year to make this trip. Her church in Germany had heard about what was going on in Toronto and she wanted to come and see for herself. During our conversation I discovered that we were staying in the same hotel. Meanwhile my husband is sitting on the floor laughing like he had heard the funniest joke EVER. It seemed as though this went on for hours. Finally he managed to pull himself together enough to get up from the floor and drive us back to the hotel. As we were riding, he could tell that I was embarrassed by his behavior so he said, "I'm sssssor" but before he could finish the sorry, whatever he found funny back at the church had resurfaced and he could hardly drive for laughing. He laughed, I PRAAAAAAAYED!!! The phrase "died laughing" took on a literal meaning. We managed to arrive back at the hotel safe and sound. Well at least one of us was sound. While Charles slept like a baby, I spent most of the night replaying the events of the evening.

The day sessions were mainly teaching and training sessions. It was the evening gatherings that were power packed. There was a steady influx of people at the hotel. Meals were spent chatting with perfect strangers and it felt so normal and nice. Everyone was so friendly, asking where we were from, what church we attended and how we had heard about Airport Vineyard Church. No one seemed to care about material things or what you did for a living. We talked mainly about God and what He was doing in our lives. Even those who were going through some difficulties were rejoicing because we all knew that even our difficulties are to strengthen us.

This is how the week progressed: I took volumes of notes, Charles went for prayer, Charles laughed, I prayed! Too soon it was Saturday, our last night in Toronto. Having traveled all those miles, I decided I would go for prayer at least this one time, unless, of course, I could come up with some reasonable, earth shattering excuse for not doing so. For example, it would be rude to stop talking to someone. When it was time for prayer, for the first time I could not find a familiar face. It seemed as though the entire church was either lined up for prayer or was part of the ministry teams. FLASHBACK! Déjà vu or whatever you want to call it, suddenly I was back to that "Kodak moment" at Covenant Church of Pittsburgh. The Spirit saying, "GO-GO" and my flesh saying, "OH-OH". It's times like this that I'm certain God has a sense of humor. Only this time I knew I wanted to be obedient. The memory of the awesome feeling of euphoria flooded my mind. We were lined up in row after row, possibly twenty-five across and ten deep. As the various teams ministered, some stood, some fell, some laid on the floor for an extended time, a few stood immediately, some knelt, some cried, some laughed but there seemed to be a transformation on every face I saw. Too soon it was my turn. There was a young lady standing in front of me who lightly touched the palms of my hands and said, "More Lord, give her more". She didn't get specific, but I knew that if it was from the Holy Spirit it would be more of something good. At that moment I felt two hands lightly on my back supporting me. I knew I was swaying a little bit but I struggled to stay on my feet. After a while, I began to relax and concentrate on receiving this "more" from the Holy Spirit. I closed my eyes so my mind would be oblivious to all that was going on around me and the next thing I knew I was in a horizontal position. I immediately opened my eyes this time. I was stuck to the floor again but this time there was not fear. The same woman who had touched my hands was now kneeling beside me. I don't remember all that she said, I just remember that they were words of encouragement. All other sounds around me seemed to be muffled but in my mind I heard these words, "Do you trust Me? Do you trust Me? Do you trust Me?" I laid on the floor for quite a while waiting to hear further words but no other words came to mind. The ride back to the hotel that evening was introspective. I began to replay all the times in the past that I had trusted God. Had we not trusted Him to teach us to raise our eight children? (Neither of us had good parent role models) Had we not trusted Him to keep our family healthy? (Most of the time raising the children we had no health insurance.) Hadn't we trusted Him for work, as my husband was self-employed? Hadn't we trusted Him to supply the means for me to go to nursing school at the age of 45? Had we not trusted him when a lump was found in my breast? Had we not trusted Him for housing and to later be able to purchase a house? Had we not trusted Him for the education of our children? I later realized that He was not asking if I had trusted Him in the past, but would I trust Him with my future?

We packed that night so we could get an early start returning home the next day. Needless to say, I did not get much sleep that night. I knew something very significant had occurred this week, but never could I have imagined how it would affect the future. The words, "Do you trust Me?" still reverberate in my mind. What did it all mean? Surely God knew whether I trusted Him or not.

Chapter III

Life has its ups and downs

Back home in Pittsburgh, I was soon into my old routine. I didn't have much time to think about the words I had heard in Toronto. My days were busy tending to my mother, who had multiple health challenges and even more emotional needs, plus answering mail (several years after Kevin's death we were still getting letters of condolences from people all around the world), returning phone calls and all the laundry that is so hard to catch up on after returning from vacation. It was weeks before those words, "Do you trust me" came to mind. At that point, those words were still a mystery.

Several month later our sister church Greater Works, was having their annual "Holy Spirit Seminar". The last evening was devoted mainly to praying for people. I got a little suspicious when I saw the familiar mats on the floor but deep in my spirit I was longing for the rest of whatever God wanted to convey to me about "trust". So there I stood, in line for prayer again. This time it was Pastor Jim's line. Pastor Jim is a very soft spoken, gentle man who co-pastured at Covenant Church of Pittsburgh. I figured I'd be safe in his line. As it became my turn to receive prayer, Pastor Jim touched my hands and prayed that God would give me more. MORE? I wasn't even sure of what I had gotten before, but before I knew it....I was on the floor. Again I was glued to the floor so I just closed my eyes and relaxed. Then I heard in my spirit only one time instead of three, "Do you trust me?" The same voice I had heard in Toronto again whispered in my spirit. As soon as I received that message I was able to get up from the floor. I got up more confused than ever. As I contemplated this over the next few months, I began to justify to God, myself and anyone else who would listen, how I had spent my life trusting God. Yet, unable to recognize that He was not asking had I trusted Him in the past, but would I trust Him in the future.

My next experience followed the same peculiar pattern. It was again during the time of our churches "Harvest Festival". My youngest son Sean, who had recently become a Christian, was home for a visit. We both decided we would go up for prayer. I wasn't surprised at his willingness to go for prayer because he had no exposure to this "falling down". Let me tell you a little bit about Sean. He is a very unique person. At birth Sean weighed 10 pounds and 10 ounces and he was 23 inches long. He was born with fontanel stenosis (he had no soft spot in his cranium). At four months he had surgery to create an open fontanel. I truly believe that during that surgery someone implanted a DayTimer organizer in Sean's brain. His first words weren't Ma-ma or Da-da but it sounded more like "Now-now". Anyone with children knows that because of the placement of the tongue, "n's" are difficult for infants to enunciate. This was not the case with Sean. Another anomaly was he cut his two top teeth before the bottom. His sister Lisa, was born a year later and he was very selective of which bottles he took from her. He never touched her milk or water bottles, only the juice. When he was a year and a half and she was six month, we would put them down for their morning naps. Soon we would hear Lisa crying. Sean would be lying in his bed with his empty bottle lying beside him and Lisa's bottle in his mouth. As soon as he saw us he'd stick the bottle back in her mouth.

It was customary for us to have "family meetings" whenever anyone felt that there was an issue that needed the entire family's attention. Sean probably called more meetings than all of his seven siblings. At the age of 6, he summoned the family for the earth shattering subject of "Could we have something other than fish sticks for Saturday dinner?" After cooking three meals a day for six days, Saturday's meal was fish and chips. Fresh fish for those who were old enough to handle the bones and fish sticks for the younger ones. Incidentally, we did change to hamburgers as a result of that meeting. Family vacations were another one of Sean's hot subjects. Needless to say, his six older brothers thought he was a pain and when I wasn't looking, he probably received numerous hits and pokes from his siblings. They nicknamed him "Mr. President". He was decorum personified. It was hardly surprising that in high school he was president of the choir, a member of the Spanish Club, the Biology Club, Sports Editor of the school newspaper, student member of the Penn Hills School Board, and on the basketball team. He loved school but disliked basketball. It was the prodding of his seventh grade gym teacher and the incentive of the possibility of an athletic scholarship that enticed him to play basketball.

Leadership came easy to Sean, but as a new Christian, being "slain in the spirit" was alien to him. He was raised in a conservative Methodist church where raising your hands to worship was considered radical and unacceptable behavior. There was one exception and that was the "mother" of the church, Hattie Bryant. She would say "let the church say "amen" and a few would break with tradition and say "amen". As a child the best part of going to church for Sean was being able to stop by the neighborhood store to buy candy on the way home. Our children were given money for Sunday School and money to buy something on the way home. I still wonder how much money actually went in the offering and how much to the corner store.

So there we stood, side by side, waiting our turn for prayer. As the Pastor approached Sean, I noticed his expression. It was easy to see that he was more than a little apprehensive. What's a mother to do? I thought, "God bless, him". Almost instantly after the Pastor touched him, he crumpled to the floor. All 6' 10" of him. He looked so funny, I started to smile, but by this time the Pastor was in front of me and before he even touched me I was on the floor. It happened so fast and to so many people we were laying in a crisscross pattern.

By this time I had learned that whatever was going on during these times, it was a pleasant experience and not something to be apprehensive about. Just a "floating on a fluffy white cloud, forget about your cares and enjoy this feeling". As I got to my feet I thought, "God, I feel so much lighter! What did I leave on the floor?" One word reverberated in my spirit as though I was in an echo chamber. PRIDE! Knowing I had heard from God, I now had to figure out what He wanted me to do with that information. Webster's dictionary says, Pride- an over high opinion of oneself; exaggerated self-esteem; conceit. Who me? Okay, now I'm sure of what it means, but what does God have to say about pride? Proverbs 8:13 describes how God hates pride and Proverbs 16:5 says it is an abomination. It was what caused Lucifer to fall from heaven (Isaiah 14:12-14).

I now know the meaning of the word and I know what God has to say about it. It also occurs to me that this "falling down" thing is not just a feel good thing but a process by which God is teaching us about ourselves. I began to look back at many areas of my life where I hadn't obeyed the tug of the Holy Spirit. Before I would have called it taking satisfaction in being right, but what is that but pride? I should always remember the most important person we have to please is God. Even now, years later, it breaks my heart to think of how pride has impeded my relationship with God. Dealing with the pride issue has caused me to be more discerning of my present actions and reactions. I've also learned that what you have been delivered from comes back to test you.

My next adventure reminded me that God has a sense of humor. I feel comfortable with most of the pastors in our church but the senior pastor use to really intimidate me. Please understand, he is known worldwide, he sings, preaches, teaches, operates in the pro-phetic, plays the piano, is involved in reconciliation world-wide, Promise Keepers, counsels other ministers, plants churches, records music and has written books. It was another one of those times when the Pastors were praying for people. The senior Pastor had left the sanctuary so I thought this was a good time to get in line. The line was growing and another Pastor said there would be a second line and it would start with me. As I walked to the front of the sanc-tuary past all those who were waiting to be prayed for, with a smile on my face like the "cat that swallowed the canary", guess who is standing at the front of this newly formed line? You got it! None other than the Senior Pastor! When you are first in line, there is no place or time for Plan B. Silently I went to my prayer language. I'm sure he knew how intimidated I was by him. It could have been my imagination but he seemed to have that same smile I had just dis-played. Was that a yellow feather floating above his head? He prayed. I perspired. Pastor touched both of my hands and very unceremoni-ously down I went. Instantly a glob of liquid gold seemed to cover my entire body. It was warm and comforting. It then shrank and became a small golden ball concentrated in my abdomen. The ball began to take on the form of a tiny baby. The baby was crying. It was a hungry, needy cry. Next, the baby grew inside me until it occu-pied half of my body. It was larger but there had been no physical change or maturity. Again the baby was crying but this time the hands and feet were flailing. It was the cry of a baby having a temper tantrum. It grew even larger. Then the baby grew until it filled my entire body but still there was no change or maturity. Slowly the baby disappeared. I lay there searching for an explanation of what this could possibly mean. Finally I whispered, "God what does all this mean?" and in my Spirit I clearly heard, "I don't send babies into battle". Instantly a sense of remorse filled my heart. I began to cry, no I think sob is more accurate, uncontrollable sobbing. To think that after almost 40 years of following Christ, in the eyes of the Holy Spirit, I was still a baby. For weeks I would start crying for no apparent reason. They were not tears caused by any particular sad or joyous event, just what seemed like bucket and buckets of tears. I would be talking to someone on the phone or out shopping and the tears would just pour. I would be scrubbing a floor or washing clothes which, before this, had never evoked tears but tedium, but now the tears would flow. I began to search the Bible for what God has to say about babies and maturity. He showed me that babies need milk and the mature require meat. I knew that, so I knew I had to dig deeper than the surface knowledge that I had. I needed life applicable, life changing knowledge as to why God saw me as a baby.

1 Corinthians 3:1-3 says "And I, brethren, could not speak to you as to spiritual men, but as to men of flesh, as to infants in Christ. I gave you milk to drink, not solid food for you were not yet able to receive it. Indeed, even now you are not yet able, for you are still fleshly. For since there is jealousy and strife among you, are you not fleshly, and are you not walking like mere men?

Hebrews 5:12-14 (NASB) says "For though by this time you ought to be teachers, you have need again for someone to teach you the elementary principles of the oracles of God, and you have come to need milk and not solid food. For everyone who partakes only of milk is not accustomed to the word of righteousness, for he is an infant but solid food is for the mature, who because of practice have their senses trained to discern good and evil". Whatever pride I left back on the church floor must have had some seedlings remaining because this sure was a humbling experience. I then asked God what all the tears were about and He directed me to Psalm 42:1-3 which says "As the deer panteth after the water brooks, so panteth my soul after thee, O God. My soul thirsteth for God, for the living God: when shall I come and appear before God? My tears have been my meat day and night, while they continually say unto me, Where is thy God?"

Chapter IV

WHERE ARE YOU GOD?

A nother reality check. Had I really doubted that God was
with me? Did I not trust God? Once more those words from
Toronto came back to me. I recognize God is trying to tell me something. It was like one shoe had dropped and I was waiting for the
other shoe. It wasn't long before the other shoe dropped. It took
the form of a bizarre betrayal, a betrayal beyond all betrayals. It was
more painful than the death of my only sibling who was murdered
in 1953 at the age of 19, more painful than the death of my second
son who died in 1991 of A.I.D.S. at the age of 35. A betrayal beyond
adultery, a betrayal beyond lies and gossip. The emotional pain was
so devastating that for days I wasn't able to eat or sleep. It was as
though I had fallen into a deep dark pit filled with razor blades and
they were cutting at the very heart of me. I did anything and everything to escape the pain. I washed clothes, I washed walls, I worked
in the yard, I screamed, I wished to die, I wished to murder. It was
a betrayal that was so shameful that even now years later it is too
painful to detail.

Then there came a time when I couldn't find a reason to do anything. I literally could not pray. I would just get on my knees and
groan. No words would come out, not even my prayer language. I

never thought of suicide, I just wanted to die. When I finally did get enough strength to go to church I would arrive late and leave as soon as service was over. I neglected my appearance, avoided my friends. One night as I lay in my bed waiting for sleep to come and rescue me from my thoughts, those words I'd heard in Toronto came blasting through the fog in my mind, "Do you trust Me?". Once more I wept uncontrollably. The same God I trusted with my eternal soul, I did not trust to get me through this time of my life. All I could say over and over was "God please forgive me". I think this simple confession broke the cycle of pain and anguish I had been experiencing and started me on the pathway of emotional and spiritual growth and healing. It was like those times when our children were small and wanted to be picked up by their earthly father and they would say "Ups Daddy, ups". Emotionally I was saying "Ups Heavenly Daddy, I need to feel the comfort and security of your arms".

Days, weeks, months went by. There were days when I would relapse into that dark morass of despair and pain. Those days became fewer and fewer, and in a world where everything seemed to be shades black and white, color now began to reappear. A sky that had appeared gray and white now was blue and white. It was as though there had been a cloud or mist over everything and suddenly a fresh wind had blown in and cleared the atmosphere. Flowers that had looked monochromatic and devoid of fragrance were again brilliant shades of pink, blue, yellow and purple. Even the white flowers were now shades of white and their fragrances exhilarating to the senses. But still in the back of my mind where I had shoved all my pain remained a torment.

Once more it was time for Greater Works annual Holy Spirit Seminar. One of the guest speakers was Gary Oliver. What a voice! I've always enjoyed his music, but that evening he also shared his testimony about the tragic loss of his son and how it had affected him and out of what seemed to be feelings of devastation, he had found new strength and direction for his life. What happened after is ingrained in my memory. He was praying for people and the line was very long. I was determined to stay as long as it took to receive prayer. I must have waited 15 minutes. I don't remember his exact words to me but in essence he said that I was entering a new season. He touched me and down I went. As I lay on the floor it was as though I was outside my body looking at myself. Inside my abdomen I saw this enormous black clump of slithering slimy stuff. It had numerous tentacles extending from it. It was hideous and terrifying.

The trip home that evening was one of silence for me. While others were sharing the marvelous word they had received, I just sat there in a quandary. By the time they got to me we were almost home and when they asked me what I had experienced, I just said "It was awesome". I wasn't ready to share about the black yucky stuff that I didn't even understand myself. I knew what had happened was significant. I knew there was more to it than what I had been able to grasp at that moment.

I was on a roll of good positive days for the next few weeks but then some event triggered something within me and I was back in a state of depression. It was then that I asked what that black yucky stuff was all about and I knew that the mass of black slimy stuff was bitterness and the tentacles were unforgiveness. I remembered that there were many, many tentacles. Some were baby tentacles, some were long. I knew forgiveness was necessary for healing and that forgiveness is an act of the will. We have to choose to forgive. Yet, I had chosen to hold on to, nurture and even make unforgiveness a comforting friend. Since then God has shown me that unforgiveness is like a splinter. It is a foreign presence in the body of a believer. If not dealt with it festers. When touched, it causes pain, affects the rest of the body, must be removed or it can cause death to all the tissue surrounding it. There is increased pain at the time of removal, then healing begins with a growth of new tissue. This new tissue is stronger than the old. Unforgiveness is that foreign body that enters the body, soul and spirit and starts its insidious process of destruction. That day, I determined to forgive everyone of everything. Especially myself. Has it been easy? NO! But I am learning to say out loud, "Father, I have needed Your forgiveness today. Help me to extend that same mercy to _____".

Chapter V

ANOTHER REALITY CHECK

I had mentioned earlier that I had a son who died from A.I.D.S. related illnesses. After his death I returned home from California and became involved in our churches outreach ministry to those living with A.I.D.S. and their families. It was through Sam Wilder, co-founder of the "Salt and Light" ministry that God allowed me to meet one of the most significant people I have ever met. Through her, I really have seen what many people living with A.I.D.S. experience. Being an actor in Hollywood allowed Kevin many privileges not afforded the average person with the disease. I met Alma Kemp (not her real name), while she was in the hospital. The social service department of the hospital had referred her to us. At that time, A.I.D.S. patients were in modified isolation so a member of the nursing staff took us into a small room where we were instructed in their infectious disease precautions. As we entered Alma's room I saw a woman who if I had passed on the street, I would have just felt sympathy for but never would of thought of as an acquaintance much less a friend. There were many scars and keloids on her face, neck and arms. Her hair was short, matted and tangled. There were as many teeth missing as present in her mouth. The ravages of substance abuse had left its destructive signature. Even more evident, though not as visible, were the emotional scars. As Alma began to speak, there was a love of life and determination deep within her that was irrepressible and contagious. Her smile made me smile. Her exuberance made me feel exuberant. We shared with her what our ministry was about and she candidly shared many things about her past. Even after spending 20 or 30 minutes with someone whose life experiences had been so unlike mine, it seemed we had known each other for years and we were just catching up on old times. Our verbal communication was different, our family arrangement was different, but our hearts were the same. I asked her about her relationship with Jesus. She said she had gone to church as a youngster and she believed in Jesus. We discussed the importance of having a personal relationship with Him. She was very excited about this so we led her in a prayer of renouncement of her past life, an acknowledgement of who Jesus is, and an acceptance of allowing Jesus to direct her future. She had shared with us one specific event in her life that she didn't think God would forgive. We assured her of His willingness to forgive her and gave her examples from the Bible where, not only had God forgiven people of this particular sin but had gone on to use them mightily. At this revelation, Alma gave us a spacious smile and a hug. We led her in a brief prayer of repentance.

Somewhere in that brief time, a bond was created between Alma and me that could only have been ordained of God. She was aware that she was living with an incurable illness, still she found a new zest for life.

Alma was transferred from the hospital to an extended care facility a few weeks later. I brought Alma a Living Bible on one of my visits. She had mentioned earlier that she hadn't read the Bible in many years because it was too difficult to understand. It became her constant companion. She would have many questions about what she had read when I visited her. She was allowed to leave this facility as long as there was someone who would be responsible for her. It was during one of weekly visits that I asked Alma if she would like to go to church with my family and me. She was reluctant to go because she didn't know how she would be received. She said she didn't have any "church clothes". I wanted to tell her that I would buy her an outfit and fix her hair, but the Holy Spirit would not let me. He said it would be an acknowledgement that she wasn't acceptable. It took many weeks of assuring her that she would be welcomed before she finally said yes. We finalized the time and the day and made arrangements with the facility to have us pick Alma up and return her.

As I was driving home, I was rejoicing at how God was moving in Alma's life, when the enemy said, "But suppose she is offended by someone, you know her clothing is rather unusual, her hair is unkempt." On and on went the negative thoughts. What had started out as a time of rejoicing was turned into a time of trepidation. I spent much of my prayer time until Sunday asking God to protect Alma from any negativity she may encounter at church and that she not change her mind about attending church. Once more not walking in the words I had heard in Toronto. Do I trust God? Sunday came and we left to pick up Alma a few minutes earlier than we had agreed on. As we entered her room, there she stood neat, clean, a cute little denim hat on her head that coordinated with her dress and with her faithful companion, The Living Bible, tucked under her arm and raring to go. That Sunday was uneventful, as were the many that followed. Alma had never been to an interracial church before or even been aware of their existence. She especially liked the praise and worship. In her words "the music was jammin!".

Alma was eventually able to leave that facility and for the first time since accepting Jesus, she would be living on her own. It was obvious that she was thrilled at the idea, but she knew that this would be a test of her ability to put her past life behind her. I was as nervous as when my oldest son decided to move out on his own. All the fears as to whether or not she was prepared to face the world. Alma found such pleasure in visiting second hand stores for furnishings. She was like a little kid in a toy store. To Alma everything was new and exciting. We gave her a few things from our house for her apartment. You would have thought that we had ordered furniture from the most exclusive furniture store in Pittsburgh. She was so appreciative of every kind and generous act shown her. Alma always brought out the best in me.

The apartment was only a few blocks from church and Alma was able to come to church frequently. We spent many days together laughing and talking and just enjoying each other. We were so different, yet so much alike. Alike in the things that really mattered. We both were brought to tears by a beautiful sunset, the sky, the smell of fresh mown grass after it rains, the smell of freshly popped popcorn. We both liked to write poetry and we would share our latest creations with each other. Differences, she liked Slim Jims. I didn't! I like anything chocolate. She didn't! Alma never graduated from high school but there was a great zest for learning and living in her. She would say "When bad things happen, you can have a pity party or just have a party. I don't like pity but I do like to party".

When we visited she always had candy for my grandson and some sort of beverage for the rest of us. She was surprised that we would allow my grandson to be around her and wanted to know whether I was concerned about his being exposed to her. I explained to her that having lost a son to A.I.D.S., I had educated myself as to how A.I.D.S. was contracted and that it wasn't spread by casual contact. Alma usually was very talkative but on one rare occasion she was quiet. I asked her what she was thinking about and she said she didn't want to die. I had no answer so I just hugged her and clung to her and allowed the tears to flow. Both hers and mine.

We would talk on the phone for hours at all hours of the day or night. I thank God for an understanding husband who never complained about the calls. I would simply mouth the words "It's Alma" and he would just roll his eyes up in his head and smile. Alma would never say "good-bye" when we hung up. She said that it sounded too final so she would always say "see ya later".

Months later Alma's medical condition began to deteriorate and the ravages of A.I.D.S. began to manifest with increased weight loss, diarrhea and loss of appetite. During one visit I noticed the smell of alcohol on Alma's breath. She admitted she had been drinking. We discussed the adverse effects of alcohol with her medicines. She said she had stopped taking her medications since they weren't doing any good and she was going to die anyway. I rarely used the word "prayer" when talking to Alma. It was obviously intimidating to her and she would say "I don't know how to pray". I would say "let's talk to Jesus" so I told her to tell Jesus how she felt. Talking to Jesus was easy for her. She spoke of all the wrong things she had been doing, and they were major. She told Jesus that she was ashamed and sorry that she had disappointed Him. She cried and asked His forgiveness. When she finished I also "talked to Jesus" and asked Him to forgive me of bad attitudes and thoughts, and words I had purposely used to hurt someone. As I prayed, I recognized my sins were just as grievous and offensive to God as were Alma's. Then I cried also.

I wish I could say that Alma had no other relapses but this was a pattern of what the following months would be. There would be times when she would call at one or two o'clock in the morning from a phone booth threatening suicide. By this time she no longer had a phone in her apartment. We would ask where she was, take her home and talk and pray with her until we felt comfortable leaving her. Numerous times I mentioned to her about talking to a professional person about the things that were bothering her but she would have none of it.

Once she called about three o'clock in the morning in intense pain from a tooth, insisting that we take her immediately to the hospital. There was no reasoning with her, so we took her to the emergency room of the local hospital. When we walked in all the people on staff knew Alma. This was not the hospital where we originally had met Alma but evidently she had visited this emergency room frequently. They were very patient and understanding and set up an appointment at the dental clinic. They were familiar with her medical situation and she openly discussed how she was doing. Alma eventually had the tooth pulled.

One night a few weeks later she again complained of a toothache at one or two o'clock in the morning. We were able to talk her into waiting the morning to take her to the hospital. When we arrived at her apartment, I asked to see which tooth was hurting. Alma had only a few teeth left and where she said the tooth was hurting there were no teeth even close. She was insistent that there were teeth there and that they were hurting. It was at this point that I recognized that Alma was using these many night excursions either because she was lonesome, afraid or was experiencing dementia which sometimes is connected to her disease.

Things went downhill from there. She would accuse people in her apartment building of stealing things from her. Her phone was disconnected and the only way I could stay in contact with her was to go to her apartment. Sometimes she would let me in. At other times I would buzz her apartment and get no answer. Occasionally she would call from a pay phone at odd hours of the night and I could tell she had been drinking. She would not tell me that she had been drinking or where she was. She would ask for prayer and I would pray but after a few minutes I could tell she was getting anxious and fearful. It was as though demons from hell were chasing her. She would abruptly say she had to go and would hang up. I would spend the rest of the night praying for her safety.

Charles and I were assigned several other families to minister to and we were speaking at churches, schools, on radio and television sharing Kevin's story. Months went by without a word from Alma. I called the hospital where I had originally met her, but she was not there. I called the other area hospitals and no one had her registered as a patient. (This was before the Right to Privacy Act).

About this time another one of those "carpet time" experiences took place. I had gone for prayer and as I lay on the floor with my eyes closed, I saw a beautiful, multicolored, shimmering butterfly. It was breathtaking! It seemed to have every color ever created in it. It fluttered around for awhile, then it flew down to the ground. When it touched the ground, it became brilliant, blinding white and flew off to the sky and out of sight. Several months later I ran into a lady who had once been a part of the A.I.D.S. ministry at our church. I learned from her that it was during the week that I had seen the butterfly, Alma had made her transition. I believe that butterfly was a symbol of Alma. I had promised to be there for Alma as she made her transition so I agonized over her leaving this world and not knowing if anyone who cared was there with her. Alma would never say goodbye when we parted or ended a phone conversation. She simply said "see ya later". So now I say those words to Alma with much love and gratitude for how she so wondrously touched and changed my life and made me a better person, so for awhile I'll say to Alma "See ya later."

Chapter VI

After The Fall

Life lessons learned since "Carpet time"

Since starting this account, I no longer struggle with the term or the experience of being "slain in the spirit", but for me a more accurate description for "slain in the spirit" is "dying to the flesh". Except for my initial experience, I believe that I had the option of resisting or falling. There were other times when I was touched and it seemed nothing happened but I know that this is a spiritual experience, which doesn't necessarily express itself in an obvious, outward manner. It is impossible to be under the power of the Holy Spirit and not be changed. The same power that spoke the earth, sun, moon, stars, universe and galaxies into existence by just saying "Let there be", and it BE, has no problem causing a 6' 2" lump of flesh and bones to be able to stand. I'd like to now share some of the life lessons learned since "carpet time".

<u>Why we need to be filled with the Holy Spirit.</u>

God reveals His plan and teaches through the Holy Spirit.
God releases power and authority through the Holy Spirit.

<u>Luke 12:12</u> "For the Holy Ghost shall teach you in the same hour what you ought to say."

<u>John 7:39</u> "But this spoke He of the Holy Spirit, which they that believe on Him should receive; for the Holy Ghost was not yet given, because that Jesus was not yet glorified."

<u>Acts 1:8</u> "But ye shall receive power after the Holy Spirit is come upon you, and ye shall be my witness unto me both in Jerusalem, and in all Judea, and in Samaria, and unto the uttermost part of the earth."

<u>1 Corinthians 2:9-16</u> "But it is written, eye hath not seen, nor ear heard, neither have entered into the heart of man, the things which God hath prepared for them that love him. But God hath revealed them unto us by His Spirit for the Spirit searcheth all things, yea, the deep things of God. For what man knoweth the things of a man which is in him? Even so the things of God knoweth no man, but the Spirit of God. Now we have received, not the spirit of the world, but the spirit which is of God; that we might know the things that are freely given to us of God. Which things also we speak, not in the words which man's wisdom teaches, but which the Holy Ghost teaches; comparing spiritual things with spiritual. But the natural man receiveth not the things of the Spirit of God: for they are foolishness to him; neither can he know them, because they are spiritually discerned. But he that is spiritual

judgeth all things, yet he himself is judged of no man. For who hath known the mind of the Lord, that he may instruct him? But we have the mind of Christ."

SIN -Admit it so you can quit it

How many times have I heard Dr. Phil say "You can't change what you don't acknowledge"?

Sin starts in the mind with a thought, then an imagination or mental picture and then an action. Hebrews 4:15 says Jesus was in all points tempted as we are, yet he was without sin. The Bible also instructs us, "Let this mind be in you, which was also in Christ Jesus (Philippians 2:5)

If you give in to sin you've lost the **battle,** but if you give up Satan wins the **war.**

Sin doesn't die, we are to die to it. We try to subdue (control, overpower, tame, tone down) the flesh but the Bible says it has to die (cease to live, vanish) but a more definitive way of expressing it is to crucify (put to death, torment) the desires of the flesh.

We want to have the penalty of sin broken Romans 6:23 (NIV) says, "the wages of sin is death but not the power of sin broken." That way we can go back and dabble in it.

Sin is disobedience to the word of God. It started in the garden. Disobedience distances us from the presence of God and delays the blessings of God. Sin separates and separates and separates until you are so far out there that is difficult to recognize the voice of God. God may, at some point turn you over to that sin (Romans 1:28) BUT if you confess and FORSAKE your sin He will remove it from us as far as the east is from the west (Psalm 103:12). God did not say as far as the north is from the south because if you go north far enough it will automatically become south. If we go east, we will continue to go east as long as we continue in the same direction. We have to choose to turn back in the old direction to our old ways. When we submit (obey, relinquish, surrender) our mind, will and emotions and walk in obedience to the Holy Spirit, He is our protection. When we grieve the Holy Spirit (walk in the flesh) the flesh becomes more vulnerable to spiritual, emotional as well as physical attacks. We are not judged by our father's sins nor are they judged for ours. "The soul who sins is the one who dies". (Ezekiel 18:4) Our behavior determines our eternal destiny. (Jeremiah 31:29,30) Whatever we give in to becomes our master. (John 8:34) The Bible has countless circumstances where Israel would

1. Fall into sin and idol worship.
2. God would cause them to be carried away into captivity or overtaken.
3. They would repent and return to God.
4. God would deliver them, by various means, and the cycle would start all over again.

The sin of rebellion was Cain's downfall. Cain was a farmer. Abel was a keeper of the sheep. It wasn't that Cain's offering wasn't perfect, it wasn't what God required. God required a blood offering. It was as if Cain said, "You want a blood offering, I'll give you a blood offering". That is why God told Cain that the ground would be cursed and he would have to roam the earth to survive. Even in rebellion he had no remorse for the killing of his brother. It was all about his punishment being more than he could bear.

The very thing the Israelites were called to sacrifice, they made an image and an idol.

Breaking the cycle of sin

1. Satan tempts you
2. You fall for it
3. Satan accused you
4. You feel guilty
5. He goes to God and accuses you
6. You go to God (confess and repent)
7. God forgives
8. Satan tempts you

The cycle begins again. We must choose to break the cycle of sin. If the devil can't make you bad, he'll make you busy. **B**eing. **U**nder. **S**atan's. **Y**oke. The devil wants you busy, God wants you fruitful. In Genesis, God told Cain that if he did well, he would be accepted. But if he did not do well, sin lies at the door. Life has always been about choices. We win or lose by what we choose. 1 Corinthians 10:13 says "There hath no temptation taken you but such is common to man, but God is faithful, who will not suffer you to be tempted above that ye are able; but will with the temptation also make a way to escape that ye may be able to bear it". Sin will remain until God destroys the source. Our maturity is evident when we break the cycle at point 1. Satan's purpose, from the beginning was to destroy God's plan. We have been reacting to attacks of the enemy. The Holy Spirit is saying don't wait for the attack, go out and take back what the enemy has stolen. We are to be proactive, not reactive. God has given us power (through the Holy Spirit) and the authority (in the name of Jesus Christ) to reclaim our homes, health, children, marriages, finances, schools, communities, nation and the world. Sin is spiritual not genetic. Certain spirits (familiar spirits) follow families and we blame it on genetics. Tay Sachs, sickle cell anemia, etc. <u>are</u> genetic. Adultery, addictions, lying, manipulation, pride, etc. are all familiar spirits. Jesus took on all of our sins past, present and future, so I know that if I resist sin it will have been one less agony Jesus had to bear on the cross.

PRAYER

Prayer is operating in the spiritual (intangible), not the physical (tangible). You can't touch a prayer but a prayer can touch you.

Prayer is a time when the Word (which represents Jesus), and Holy Spirit (which is in us) and the person have fellowship. Prayer is a time for listening as well as speaking, as in any relationship. Who better can we listen to than the Holy Spirit. Eloquent prayers touch the heart of man; ardent (fervent, effectual) prayers reach the heart of God.

A powerful pray-er's words reaches the ears of God and changes the hearts of mankind. Prayer is POWERFUL! We've confused prestige with power. Prestige is the ability to impress or influence because of success or wealth. Power is the ability to do, to act, to cause change; authority. All power has to have a source. Holy Ghost power causes demons to flee, the lame to walk, the blind to see, people to give up their addictions, marriages to be restored.

Prayer gives God the legal right to move on our behalf. Nations fall into poverty because they forget God. (Deuteronomy 8:18-20) Sometimes God calls an entire nation to pray, sometimes a select group of people, sometimes an individual but prayer is never an option. It is our obedience not our size or strength that effects change.

We have the ability to pray storms of life away but most storms catch us unaware. In the storm we must be guided by the voice of the Lord and His Word. Do not look to the left or the right, don't stop, and don't look back. Continue to move in the direction of His voice.

God gives us a word. Satan puts up what looks like a brick wall (obstacles) in front of us. He is so clever that we believe what we see instead of what the Word says. We just see the wall and feel defeated. We have to realize that the wall, like Satan, is only an imitation of the real thing. We have been deceived! If we come against the wall we find that it's as phony as Satan. It's made of tissue paper. Often one prayer, or the Word spoken, will tear it down. Ask Joshua (Joshua 6). No matter what you are going through, God will either get you out of it as He did Lot (Genesis 19), protect you in it, as He did the Israelites during the institution of the Passover (Exodus 12), or take you through it.

We, as a nation must wage war in the natural with strategies, weapons, planes, ships and smart bombs. As Christians, in our battles, our weapon is PRAYER. "The weapons of our warfare are not carnal, but mighty through God to the pulling down of strongholds". (2 Corinthians 10:4) After we have put on our loins truth, our feet peace, taken up the shield of faith, donned the helmet of salvation, and taken up the Word which is the sword of the Spirit, we are instructed to PRAY always with all supplication in the Spirit. (Ephesians 6:14-18)

Our prayer language is a gift. If you don't have one, just ask and speak. It's that easy! The key is to ASK. God told Solomon to "Ask what I shall give thee". (1 Kings 3:5, 2 Chronicles 1:7). To David He said "Ask of me and I shall give you the heathen for thine inheritance and the uttermost parts of the earth for thy possession". (Psalm 2:8) To Ahaz "Ask thee a sign of the Lord, thy God; ask it either in the depth, or in the height above". (Isaiah 7:11) Jesus said "Ask, and it shall be given you...(Matthew 7:7) "Whatsoever you ask in prayer, believing you shall receive." (Matthew 21:22, 1 John 3:22, 5:14,15; John 14:13,14; John 15:7; James 1:5,6) "Now unto Him who is able to do exceedingly abundantly above all we can ASK or think, according to the power that worketh in us." (Ephesians 3:20)

What an honor and privilege to converse with the creator of all that is created, acknowledging God's mighty presence in all the earth, the vastness of the universe that is beyond all comprehension with its billions upon billions of stars in billions upon billions of galaxies and God has named each one of them. Yet He sees a sparrow when it falls. How much more He must love and care for us who were created in His likeness. He loved us so much He sent His only son to die for our sins.

FORGIVE AND FORGET

Forgiveness is the act of pardoning someone of their wrongdoing. Forgiveness is releasing a person from the penalty. Forgetting means to remove the blame. To choose to no longer connect the person (God's creation) to the offense (the devil's creation). Forgetting doesn't mean no longer remembering, but not allowing the offense the power to influence future decisions. Not allowing their past behavior to influence your present or future behavior. Forgetting means never bringing it up again. Unforgiveness is a major sin and has devastating repercussions. God said if we don't forgive others, He won't forgive us. (Matthew 6:15; Mark 11:25; Matthew 18:21-35; Colossians 3:13) Yet too few sermons are preached on forgiveness. Jesus, the perfect one, thought it expedient to say on the cross "Father, forgive them". (Luke 23:34) That's how important forgiving is. It's not the letting go that hurts, it's the holding on that is devastating. If we don't forgive, we won't forget! We are all living stones and God is in the process of building His church and the gates of hell will not be able to stand against us. Stone upon stone we are being positioned, with Jesus as our cornerstone. We must align the building of our lives with the cornerstone. When we chip away at each other we are making the stones unable to fit properly in their assigned positions. When we don't align ourselves with the Word of God, we allow gaps in the building and the enemy is able to come in and weaken the foundation.

ARMOUR AND ARMOUR BEARERS

Many years ago, as part of my morning routine, I was mentally putting on my armor, according to Ephesians 6:11, when the Holy Spirit said, "When did I tell you to take it off? This is a twenty-four hour a day battle. My armor is not cumbersome. It is spiritual, not physical garments because the battle is spiritual. When you put on salvation (are saved, give your life to the Lord, are born again), righteousness and truth are to become a part of you, wherever you go. peace should follow; your faith shall be your protection and My word shall be your weapon". God has given us the protection and the weapons for warfare. He's done His part. We are prepared for battle but are we fit for war? Gideon had to separate those who were not fit.

I've seen many men and women of God who walk into an assembly with an entourage of people carrying their Bible, water, books, tapes, etc. I wondered why. When I would enquire of my more enlightened friends they would tell me that they were "Armor Bearers". This reminds me of a more recent situation regarding armor and armor bearers. There are two very significant women in my life. One is Karen Garland and the other is Marette Simpson. They had started a ministry and I became a frequent follower of their ministry. One is a Pastor and the other is an Evangelist. I am an intercessor but I thought the Holy Spirit was saying "armor bearer". Surely God in His infinite wisdom wasn't asking me who, has frequent senior moments, uses a cane to walk and a pacemaker to keep the old ticker ticking, to carry books, water, etc. What was more confusing the two of them went in different directions. I was really confused. I thought "God did I miss you on this?" He took me on a journey through the Word and revealed some things to me. Armor bearer is one who spends time in intercessory prayer, fasting and speaking the Word over someone. 2 Corinthians10:3-4 says "For though we walk in the flesh, we do not <u>war</u> after the flesh. For the weapons of our warfare are not carnal, but mighty through God to the pulling down of strongholds." Okay, so now I know that armor bearing isn't something you can touch but something that touches the heart of God. Next He directed me to Hebrew 4:12, "For the <u>word</u> of God is quick, and powerful and sharper than any two edged sword, piercing even to the dividing asunder of soul and spirit, and of the joints and marrow, and is a discerner of the thoughts and intents of the heart". Ephesians 6:11 says to "Put on (cover oneself with or take on) the whole armor of God". We are to wear truth, righteousness, peace, salvation and ABOVE ALL faith. I asked "Why above all faith?" and the answer was "Satan may not know your assignment but He does recognize and is repelled by your faithfulness." I was still not quite sure why fasting was included. He took me to <u>Acts</u> 14:23 (NIV) "Paul and Barnabas appointed elders for them in each church and with prayer and <u>fasting</u>, committed them to the Lord in whom they put their trust". While these scriptures are familiar, they take on a new dimension and they literally come alive when they are applied to everyday life situations. Final answer? Armor is not for the physical but the spiritual and an armor bearer is not a person who carries your Bible, books water, etc. but one whom God has designated for you to carry that person in prayer, fasting and speaking the Word over them. So I ask "Who are those people who carry the Bibles, books, water etc. and the Holy Spirit said "They are people who carry Bibles, books, water etc."

THE POWER OF OUR WORDS

Speech is powerful! God spoke the world into existence. I believe being created in "God's image" is somehow connected with our ability to communicate with Him. In Matthew 17:20, Jesus said "if ye have faith as a grain of mustard seed, you shall SAY to this mountain remove hence to yonder place and it shall remove, and nothing shall be impossible unto you". In Numbers 20:7 God told Moses to SPEAK to the rock. Mark 4:39, Jesus SPOKE the Word to Satan. In Matthew 12:36,37 Jesus says "But I say unto you, that every idle word that men shall SPEAK, they shall give account of in the day of judgment. For by thy words thou shalt be condemned". Even the unpardonable sin is something spoken not something done. (Luke 12:10) BE CAREFUL WHAT YOU SPEAK!!!!!

PRAISE vs. WORSHIP

> John 4:23,24 "But the hour cometh and now is, when the true worshipers shall worship the Father in spirit and in truth; for the Father seeketh such to worship Him. God is a spirit, and they that worship Him must worship Him in spirit and in truth."

> Exodus 34:14 "For thou shalt worship no other god, for the Lord whose name is Jealous is a jealous God."

We praise with our lips.
We worship with our Spirit.

Praise is an outer court experience.
Worship is a holy of holies experience.

Praise can be devoid of personal relationship.
Worship requires relationship, intimacy.

We can praise people's talents.
We are to worship God alone.
The unsaved can praise God but not worship. Worship exists because of relationship.

There is a point in praise when praise becomes worship and no longer an offering of praise but it is a one to one relationship.

Worship is when the Spirit of God which is in you connects with the God of the Spirit.

WISDOM

James 3:17 says:

Wisdom is:

PURE-righteousness, cleanness, sanctification, absence of immorality, holiness.

PEACE-rest, calmness, absence of torment, fear, worry, confusion, anxiety, cares.

A state of resting in God that is untouchable. A state of rest that no trial or circumstances can penetrate.

GENTLE-Kindness, compassion. The absence of harshness, rudeness, violence, roughness, especially in words, behavior and actions.

EASY TO BE INTREATED-humility, meekness, teachable, lowliness of mind, The absence of pride, stubbornness.

MERCY AND GOOD FRUITS-love, joy, peace long-suffering, gentleness, goodness, faith, meekness, temperance (Galatians 5:22,23)

WITHOUT PARTIALITY - equality, rich or poor, Jew or Gentile.

WITHOUT HYPOCRISY - truth at all cost, full of integrity and honesty.

> Psalms 111:10 (NIV) says "The fear of the Lord is the beginning of wisdom; all who follow His precepts have good understanding. To him belongs eternal praise".

> Matthew 11:19 (NIV) says "wisdom is proved right by her actions".

> James 1:5 (NIV) says "If any of you lacks wisdom, he should ask God, who gives generously to all without finding fault, and it will be given to him".

Intellect and knowledge can come from many sources but wisdom comes only from God. I believe the prayers and the decisions made by the body of Christ, will not only determine our future but will in many ways, alter the course of history.

Jesus' last words were, Acts 1:9 (NIV) "But you shall receive power, after the Holy Spirit is come upon you; and you shall be witnesses unto me both in Jerusalem, and in all Judea, and in Samaria, and unto the uttermost part of the earth." That doesn't just mean we are to tell about Him, but we are also to do the works that He did. That is the purpose of the power that we have received. Proverbs 23:23 states "Buy the truth and sell it not, also WISDOM and instruction, and understanding." In other words, find out what is true and live our lives by that standard. Too often we become excessively focused on the daily struggles of paying bills, raising children and meeting other financial and emotional responsibilities (which are necessary) but neglect the purpose for which we were born. God knew the circumstances of our birth as well as the purpose. We are instructed in Proverbs 23:4 "Labor not to be rich and to cease from our own wisdom." The Bible tells us to, "seek first the kingdom of God and His righteousness, an all these things will be added." (Matthew 6:33) How do we seek the kingdom? Through prayer and fasting. By prayer I mean talking to AND listening to God. We should spend more time listening to hear what God has to say. He already knows what we need and how we feel, but do we know what He wants of us? Prayer is a two-way conversation. Sometimes He speaks through the Bible, sometimes, through others, and sometimes through our just being silent and waiting on His guidance. Psalms 37:7 says "to rest in the Lord, and wait patiently for Him." Waiting is not always easy but once you've heard from God it is always worth the wait. There is something worse than waiting for God, and that is wishing you had.

Fasting is denying the natural man and feeding the spiritual man. Abstaining from things that give pleasure to the body and soul such as food, TV, printed media, social media, computers, hobbies and sometimes even people. In Song of Solomon 2:10 it says, "My beloved spake, and said to me, "Rise up, my love, my fair one, and come away". Though Solomon was speaking in the natural, I believe in the supernatural it is also speaks to the body of Christ. Christ is saying, "I want your undivided attention, just the two of us.

There are some things for our ears only." Once you have had those times of intimacy in His presence, you never forget them and you long for more.

Our decisions should be made according to the word of God and not our mental reasoning. Seek the wisdom of the one who was, and is and is to come. He was wise enough to create the entire universe, surely He can handle what is facing us in the days to come.

Chapter VII

A STRING OF "PEARLS"
FROM THE SEA OF LIFE.

M any years have past since I had my first experience with the controversial occurrence of being slain in the spirit. I'm obviously now a believer and have spiritually progressed in various ways. Here are a few pearls of wisdom I have learned in the process.

- A Rock (stones)- The significance of the insignificant.
  We are impressed by diamonds, emeralds, sapphires, rubies, etc. We should get more excited about ROCKS.
  God started with a rock (the earth).
  The first man was made from a rock. (The soil) The Church is called a rock with Jesus as the chief cornerstone.

  — Daniel 2:34-35. In Nebuchadnezzar's dream, God cut out a rock to turn a statue made of gold, silver, bronze, iron and clay into dust.
  — 1 Samuel 17:49. It was a rock that struck down Goliath.

— Numbers 20:8. God told Moses to speak to a rock and it brought forth enough water for all of the people and their flocks.

— Deuteronomy 32:4b(NIV). Moses sang "He is the rock, His works are perfect and all His ways are just..."

— Psalms 61:2,3 (NIV). David prayed "From the ends of the earth I call to you, I call as my heart grows faint; lead me to the rock that is higher than I for you have been my refuge, a strong tower against the foe."

— Matthew 16:18. Jesus changed Simon's name to Peter (which means rock)

— Exodus 4:25. A sharp stone was used to cut away the foreskin.

— Genesis 31:44-46 (NIV). "Come now, let's make a covenant, you and I, and let it serve as a witness between us". So Jacob took a stone and set it up as a pillar. He said to his relatives, "Gather some stones." So they took stones and piled them in a heap, and they ate there by the heap." Stones were used a sign of a covenant.

— Genesis 35:14 (NIV). "Jacob set up a stone pillar at the place where God had talked with him,...." So basically:

- The Ten Commandments were carved from rock.
- Peter was known as the Rock
- Rocks were used for stoning people to death.
- Rocks were used for building.
- Rocks were used as memorials.

- In Daniel 2:34, it was a rock that crushed the statue.
- David felled Goliath with a rock.
- Jesus is referred to as the chief cornerstone.

- TIME--(A created entity. <u>Genesis</u> 1:1 (NIV) says, "In the beginning God created the heavens and the earth." Before He created the heavens and the earth, He had to create time.) It is no problem for God to reverse time. It is as easy for Him to reverse time as it is for us to turn our watch backwards or push the fast forward button on a V.C.R. There are times when we are in the presence of God that time seems to disappear. Times when it's difficult to tell whether we have been in His presence five seconds, five minutes or five hours.

- Jesus was selective but not exclusive. Jesus selected 12 men but He also said "Come unto me ALL who are heavy laden".

- The keys to releasing the anointing is repentance and obedience.

- God's timing is perfect. Worship and work while you're waiting because whatever God promised, He WILL do. Noah was 600 years old when he entered the ark. Abraham waited many years for the child God promised. Joseph waited about 30 years for his dream to be fulfilled. Moses was 80 years old when he led the people out of Egypt. Even Jesus waited 30 years before He started His ministry.

- Most of our struggles revolve around wanting something we don't have or having something we don't want.

- The power isn't in the armor of God but in the God of the armor.

- Life is not always fair but God is always faithful.

- Jesus' birth divided history. Even the most devout atheist HAS to acknowledge Jesus every time they write a check or anything else that requires a date.
- Courage is not the absence of fear but the mastery of it.
- Jesus will give us the desires of our hearts when HE becomes the desire of our hearts. (Matthew 6:33 "But seek ye first the kingdom of God, and His righteousness and all these things shall be added unto you")[1]
- To be "set on high above all nations" (Deuteronomy 28:1) means to have the favor of God.
- Sometimes God doesn't immediately answer is because we have drifted away from Him and He wants to draw us closer.
- Whatever you give in to becomes your master. (John 8:34)
- From those who are talkative seek knowledge. From those who are quiet seek wisdom.
- The same tools that Jesus used most of His life are the same tools that were used to end His life.
- Each day is a lesson and a blessing.
- Eternal issues cannot be measured (viewed) by earthly (human) standards. We cannot always see the big picture but there IS a big picture. The disciples of Jesus couldn't understand His death. What looked like loss was mankind's greatest victory.
- Our Christianity is a partnership. God chooses what we go through. We choose how we go through it.
- If God inhabits our praises, who inhabits our complaining?
- We all are saved to serve.
- The Bible teaches us to live like THE king, not like A king.
- Satan can't take what you give to God.

1

- God owes us nothing but He has given us everything.
- Have you ever read the Bible and got a deeper meaning of the same scripture? It's because the Word of God is alive! As we mature in the Lord, He takes us to a broader dimension.
- Refuse to receive any word that doesn't come from God.
- God has called us to be "salt and light" (Matthew 5:13) Salt seasons, causes healing, preserves, brings out the best in whatever it touches. Light brings clarity, defines and illuminates its surroundings and shows the way.
- The ability to grow spiritually is contingent on the ability to die to self. Spiritual maturity is first Esteeming earthly things lightly Hebrews 11:24-27, next being dead to praise or criticism 1 Corinthians 4:3-4, and finally the ability to hear God clearly and obey quickly.
- If you want an opinion, ask someone. If you want a solution, ask God.
- We carry the presence of God in us.
- There are no gray areas in God. Things are black or white, good or bad.
- Success-Success is not what God has done for me, but what He has done through me. We are God's vessels. We are to be filled up to be poured out.
- Simply put, wisdom is doing things God's way.
- There are many ways to hell but only one way to heaven.
- Don't ask God to strengthen you, ask Him to be your strength. Don't operate in the "me" but in the "He".
- Satan roars. God whispers.
- God's words were spoken so they could be written, and they were written so that they could be spoken.
- An altar call is a marriage between you and God.
- Our decisions define our destiny.

- Whatever I'm going through, God has either permitted it or purposed it.
- Negative thoughts affect you. Negative words affect others.
- Lord, help me to let go of yesterday so that I may take hold of today. Then help me to get past me to You.
- God created pain as a warning signal. It's the cause of the pain, not the pain that is the issue.
- Church-Its purpose is not about people going to church as much as the Church going to the people.We come together to be equipped, encouraged and instructed to go out and do the work of the Lord. WE are the Church. We meet in a building.
- I don't know my future so I put NO trust in it. I do know my God so I put ALL my trust in Him.
- To prove His love, Christ died for me. To prove my love, I live for Him.
- Every problem has a purpose and a promise.
- If God is who He says He is, and He can do what He says He can, and I am who He says I am, then "I can do all things through Christ who strengthens me." (Philippians 4:13)

Trying to figure Jesus out can be mind-blowing.

- He was smitten and yet He is esteemed.
- He was a servant and the King of Kings.
- He was meek and lowly yet He is high and Lifted up.
- He is the Lion of Judah yet He is the Lamb of God.
- He was without sin yet He bore the sins of the world.
- He is the Alpha and Omega, the beginning and the end, yet He has no beginning or end. Plus the benefits of living

according to God's word is forgiveness, healing, redemption, love and mercy and so much more. (Psalm 103)
-    He divides to multiply.

I don't have all the answers to what life is all about, but I do have a personal relationship with the one who has all the answers. God has a plan and a purpose for everyone's life. This journey called "life" is about finding and fulfilling that plan and purpose. How can we know the plan without knowing the planner which is God? All I can say is, He is who He says He is, and He says:

I AM

- Your shield (Genesis 5:)
- The Almighty God (Genesis 17:1)
- The God of Abraham....(Genesis 26:24)
- I am, that I am (Exodus 3:14)
- The Lord Jehovah (Exodus 6:2)
- The Lord that healeth thee (Exodus 15:26)
- A jealous God (Exodus 20:5)
- Gracious (Exodus 22:27)
- Holy (Leviticus 11:44,45)
- God (Psalms 46:10)
- The Lord; that is my name (Isaiah 43:8)
- Your God, your Savior, the Holy One (Isaiah 43:3)
- He that blotted out sins (Isaiah 43:25)
- The first and the last and beside me there is no God (Isaiah 44:6)
- The God of Israel (Isaiah 45:3)
- The Lord that maketh all things (Isaiah 44:24)
- Your Comforter (Isaiah 51:12)

- The Lord and there is none else (Isaiah 45:5,6)
- Advocate (1 John 2:1)
- Almighty (Revelation 1:8)
- Author and finisher of our faith (Hebrews 12:2)
- The bread of life (John 6:35)
- Counselor (Isaiah 9:6)
- Deliverer (Romans 11:26)
- Everlasting Father (Isaiah 9:6)
- The first and the last (Revelations 1:17)
- The Good Shepherd (John 10:11)
- The Great High Priest (Hebrews. 4:14)
- The Holy One (Acts 3:14)
- Immanuel-God with us (Isaiah 714)
- The Just One (Acts 7:52)
- King of the ages (1Timothy 1:17)
- King of Kings, Lord of Lords (1Timothy 6:15)
- Light of the world (John 8:12)
- Lion of the tribe of Judah (Revelation 5:5)
- Lord of all (Acts 10:36)
- Mediator (1Timothy 2:5)
- Truth (John 1:14)
- The Word of God (Revelation 19:13)
- Only begotten Son (John 1:18)
- Prince of Peace (Isaiah 9:6)
- Redeemer (Job 19:25)
- Resurrection and life (John 11:25)
- Savior (Luke 2:11)
- Son of David (Matthew 1:1)
- Son of God (Matthew 2:15)
- Son of man (Matthew 8:20)

A string of "pearls" from the sea of life.

JESUS HE WOULD RATHER DIE THAN LIVE
WITHOUT YOU.

WILL YOU TRUST HIM?

The End

CPSIA information can be obtained
at www.ICGtesting.com
Printed in the USA
BVHW031121030322
630567BV00003B/119